Simple Machines

Wedges
and ramps

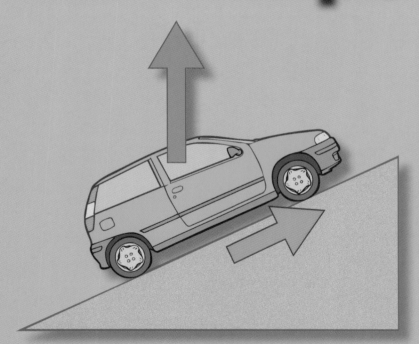

Chris Oxlade

FRANKLIN WATTS
LONDON•SYDNEY

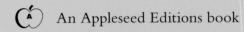 An Appleseed Editions book

First published in 2007 by Franklin Watts

Franklin Watts
338 Euston Road, London NW1 3BH

Franklin Watts Australia
Hachette Children's Books
Level 17/207 Kent St, Sydney, NSW 2000

© 2007 Appleseed Editions

Created by Appleseed Editions Ltd,
Well House, Friars Hill, Guestling,
East Sussex TN35 4ET

Designed by Helen James
Edited by Mary-Jane Wilkins
Artwork by Bill Donohoe

ISBN 978 0 7496 7569 1

Dewey Classification: 621.8

A CIP catalogue for this book is available from the British Library.

Picture credits
page 5 Jim Zuckerman/Corbis; 6 Keren Su/Corbis; 10 Hein van den
Heuvel/Zefa/Corbis; 12 Rosa & Rosa/Corbis; 15 Jim Craigmyle/Corbis;
16 Chris Oxlade; 17 Jessica Rinaldi/Reuters/Corbis; 18 Klaus Hackenberg/
Zefa/Corbis; 20 Helmut Mayer Zur Capellen/Zefa/Corbis; 21 Linda
Richardson/Corbis; 22 Maurice Nimmo; Frank Lane Picture Agency/Corbis;
23 Michael Nicholson/Corbis; 28 Ben Le/Corbis; 29 Laureen March/Corbis

Printed in China

Franklin Watts is a division of Hachette Children's Books

Contents

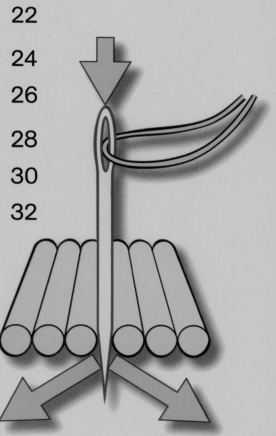

What is a simple machine?

A simple machine is something that helps you do a job. We use simple machines to help us every day. Here are some simple machines you might have at home.

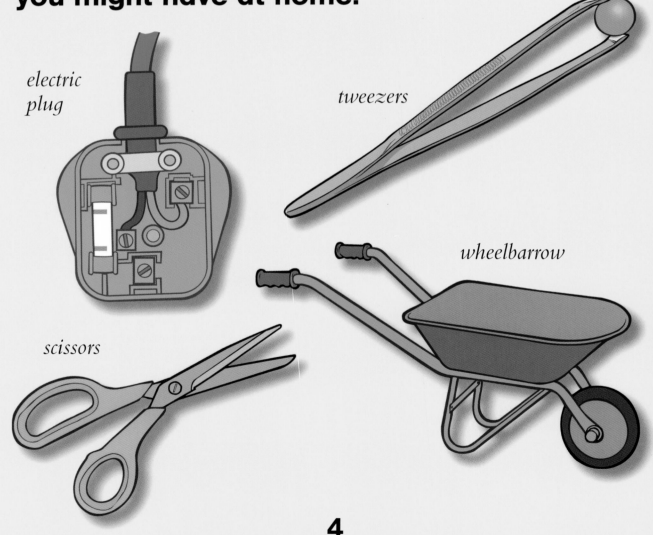

electric plug

tweezers

wheelbarrow

scissors

This book is about simple machines called wedges and ramps.

The head of an axe is a wedge. We use an axe to cut wood. A ramp is like a wedge. It helps to lift things.

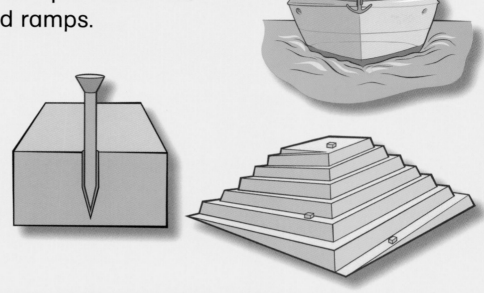

The head of an axe is wedge-shaped.

Pushes and pulls

You push on a wedge to make it work. When you push, the wedge makes a push, too. Scientists call all pushes and pulls forces.

This chisel is a wedge. A stonemason shapes stone with it.

We show pushes and pulls with arrows. The arrow points in the direction the force is pushing or pulling. The longer the arrow the bigger the push or pull.

Red arrows show pushes and pulls.

Blue arrows show movement.

This force arrow shows that the person's feet are pushing down on the ground.

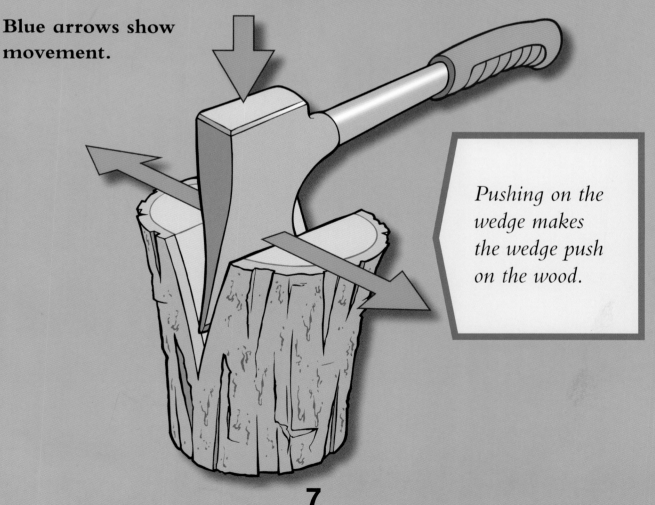

Pushing on the wedge makes the wedge push on the wood.

How wedges and ramps work

A wedge is a very simple machine. It is made from hard material, such as wood, plastic or metal. From the side it is shaped like a triangle.

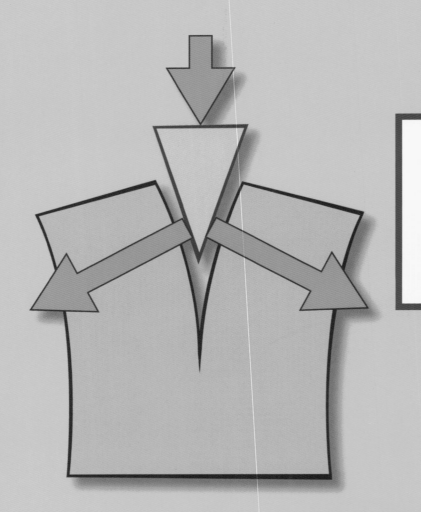

A wedge changes the direction of a push. It makes the push larger, too.

A ramp is like a wedge lying on the ground. A ramp doesn't move. Instead, you push something up it. This is easier than lifting the object straight upwards.

Pushing an object up a ramp is a way of lifting it higher.

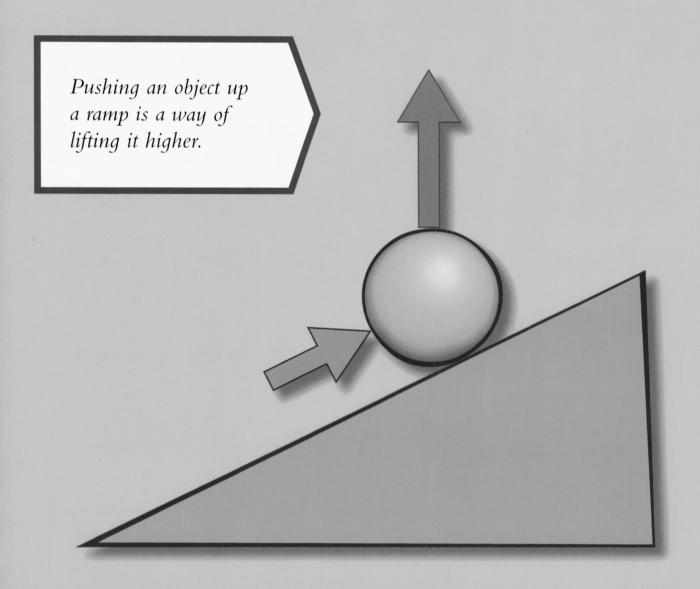

Cutting with wedges

**We use wedges to cut materials.
A pizza cutter has a wedge
around the outside of the wheel.**

You press the pizza cutter down and
roll it along. The wedge cuts the pizza
and pushes the pieces apart.

*A pizza cutter
works like a knife
that rolls along.*

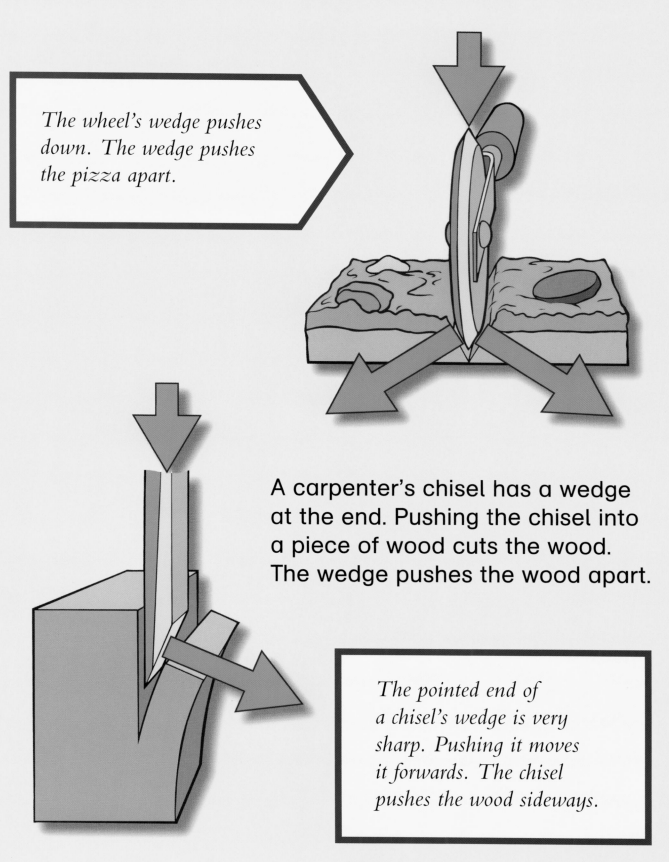

The wheel's wedge pushes down. The wedge pushes the pizza apart.

A carpenter's chisel has a wedge at the end. Pushing the chisel into a piece of wood cuts the wood. The wedge pushes the wood apart.

The pointed end of a chisel's wedge is very sharp. Pushing it moves it forwards. The chisel pushes the wood sideways.

Piercing with wedges

We use wedges to pierce materials, and to make holes.

The sharp point of a nail is a wedge.
The wedge pushes wood to the side
as the nail is hammered in.

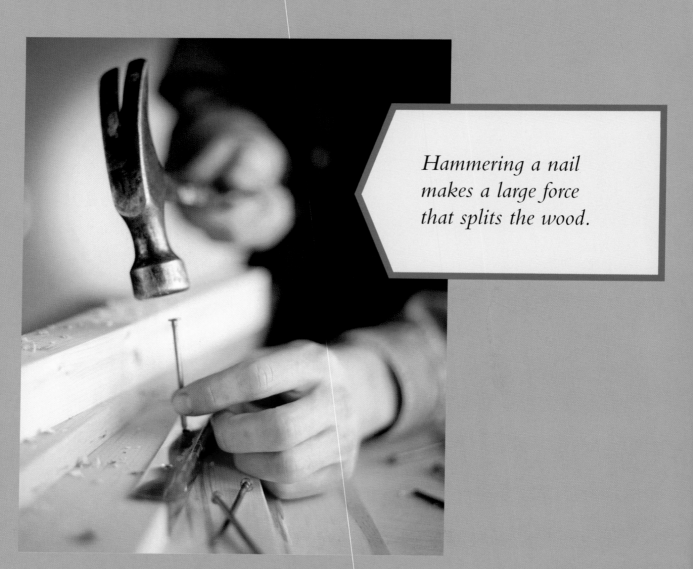

*Hammering a nail
makes a large force
that splits the wood.*

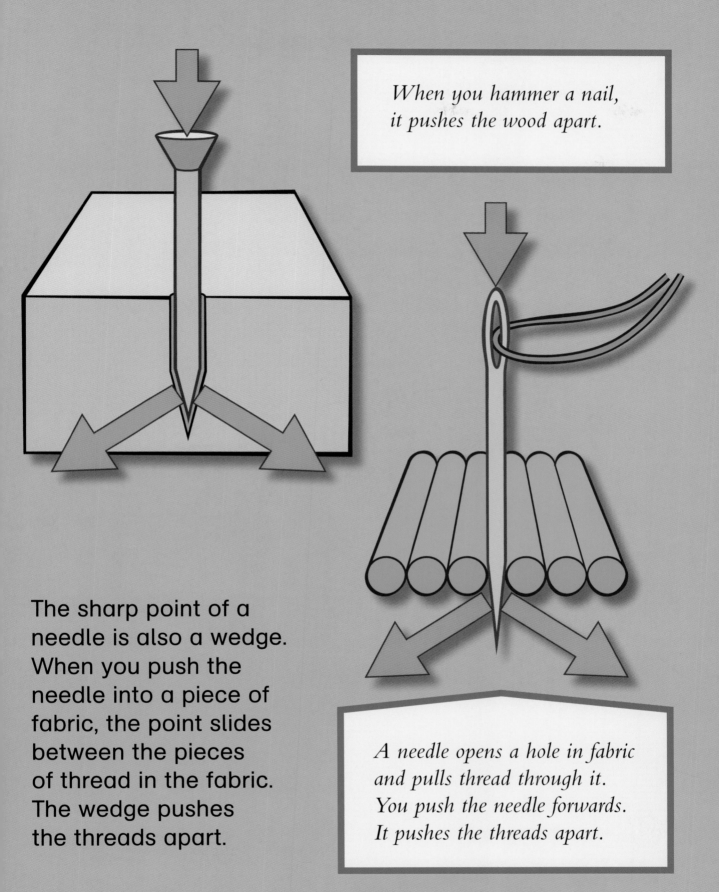

The sharp point of a
needle is also a wedge.
When you push the
needle into a piece of
fabric, the point slides
between the pieces
of thread in the fabric.
The wedge pushes
the threads apart.

A needle opens a hole in fabric
and pulls thread through it.
You push the needle forwards.
It pushes the threads apart.

Gripping with wedges

We can jam wedges into gaps, to grip things and stop them moving.

A door wedge holds a door open when we jam it between the door and the floor.

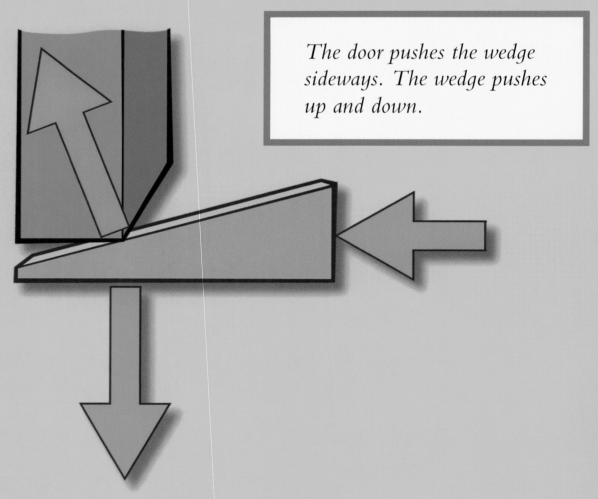

The door pushes the wedge sideways. The wedge pushes up and down.

Carpenters use wedges in joints between pieces of wood. A wedge jams the pieces tightly together so that they can't move apart.

A carpenter puts together a dovetail joint. There are two wedges in the middle.

Lifting with ramps

We use ramps to move things upwards.

A loading ramp makes it easier to move heavy things up on to a vehicle. It would be much harder to lift the things straight upwards.

A digger being loaded on to a trailer. The digger is driving up a ramp.

A wheelchair ramp allows people who use wheelchairs to get into a building from the pavement. The ramp has a very gentle slope so that people can push themselves up it.

This person uses a ramp to get up to his front door.

The person pushes on the chair's wheels. The ramp makes the chair move upwards.

More ramps

We use ramps on paths, roads and railways. Ramps make it easier to move up hills.

A zigzag path is a ramp that makes it easier to walk up a steep hill. Going straight up a hill is much harder.

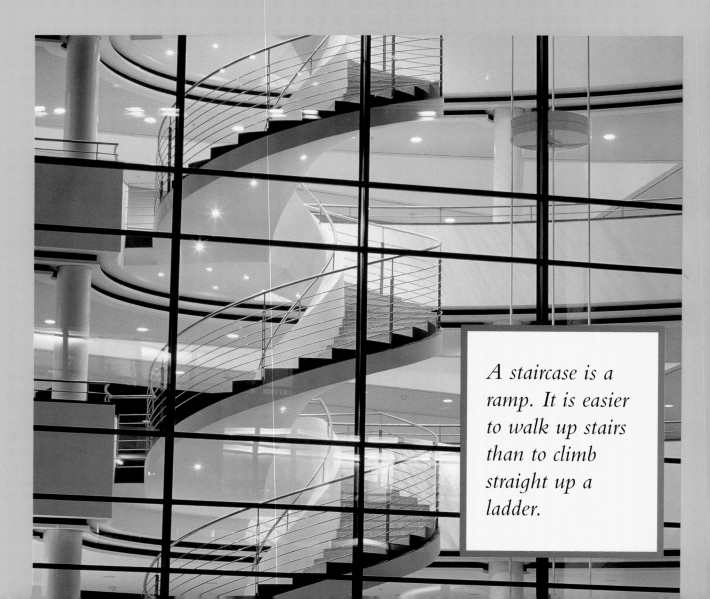

A staircase is a ramp. It is easier to walk up stairs than to climb straight up a ladder.

Walking along a zigzag path is easier, but you have to walk further.

Most cars and trucks can't go up very steep hills. Their engines cannot make enough push, and their wheels slip. They need ramps to climb upwards.

The car's wheels push the car forwards. The ramp makes the car move upwards.

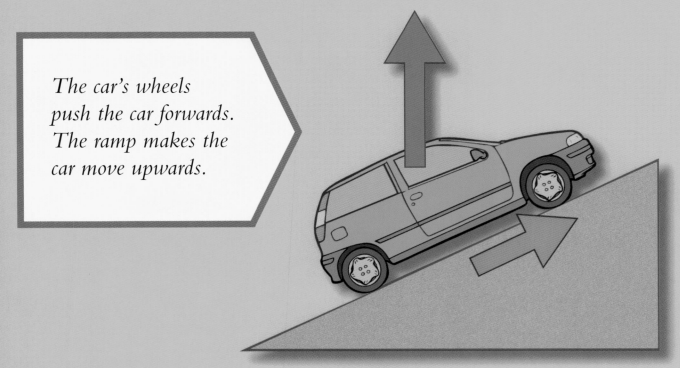

19

Wedges and ramps in machines

Complicated machines often use wedges and ramps to work.

A digger's bucket uses wedges to break up the soil. The bucket has wedge-shaped teeth at the front.

A digger bucket's teeth split the soil apart as the bucket digs in.

20

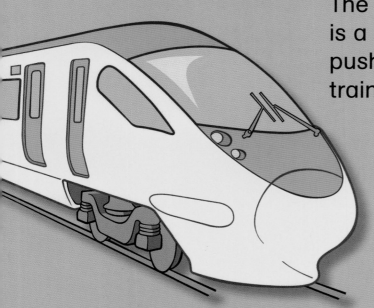

The front of a high-speed train is a wedge shape. The wedge pushes the air aside as the train speeds along the track.

A train's wedge-shaped nose pushes air up and over the train.

A quarry conveyor moves crushed rock into the top of a hopper. The conveyor is a ramp.

This conveyor lifts heavy rocks. It would need more force to lift the rocks straight upwards.

Wedges and ramps in the past

People have been using wedges and ramps for thousands of years.

The wedge was one of the first tools that people used. They made wedge-shaped cutting tools and arrow heads by chipping stones into shape.

A cutting tool made from a hard stone called flint.

The plough was invented thousands of years ago. The first ploughs were simple wedge-shaped pieces of wood which broke up the soil so that seeds could be planted.

Builders used ramps before cranes were invented. The Egyptians built huge ramps to move the giant stone blocks for their pyramids.

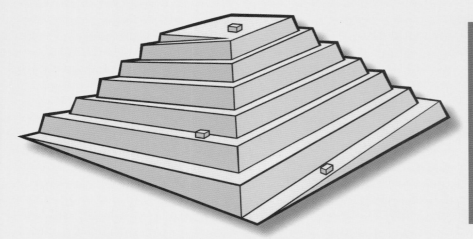

Teams of Egyptian workers hauled stones up the ramps.

Fun with wedges and ramps

On the next four pages are some activities for you to do. They will help you to understand how wedges and ramps work.

TESTING A WEDGE

You will need:

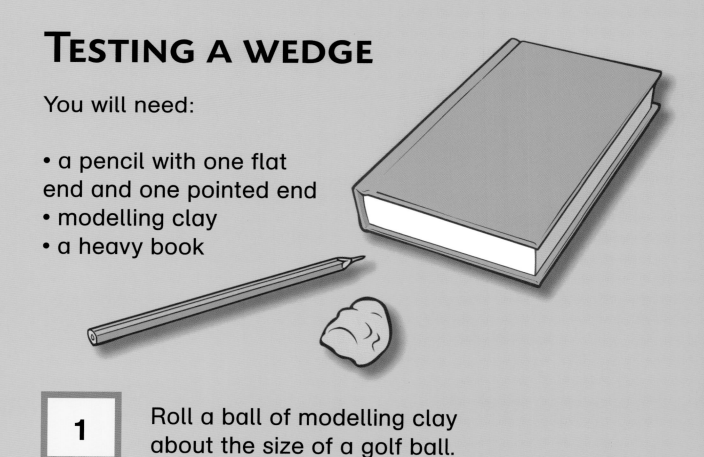

- a pencil with one flat end and one pointed end
- modelling clay
- a heavy book

1 Roll a ball of modelling clay about the size of a golf ball.

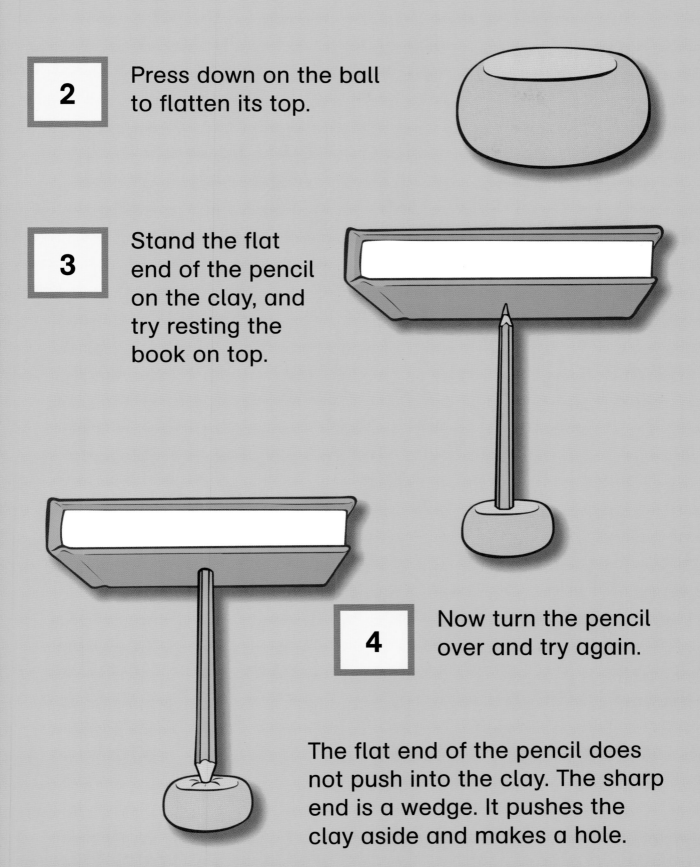

2 Press down on the ball to flatten its top.

3 Stand the flat end of the pencil on the clay, and try resting the book on top.

4 Now turn the pencil over and try again.

The flat end of the pencil does not push into the clay. The sharp end is a wedge. It pushes the clay aside and makes a hole.

Sliding up a ramp

You will need:

• a thin elastic band
• a piece of string
(about 50 cm long)
• a large book and
some small books
• a small, heavy object,
such as stapler

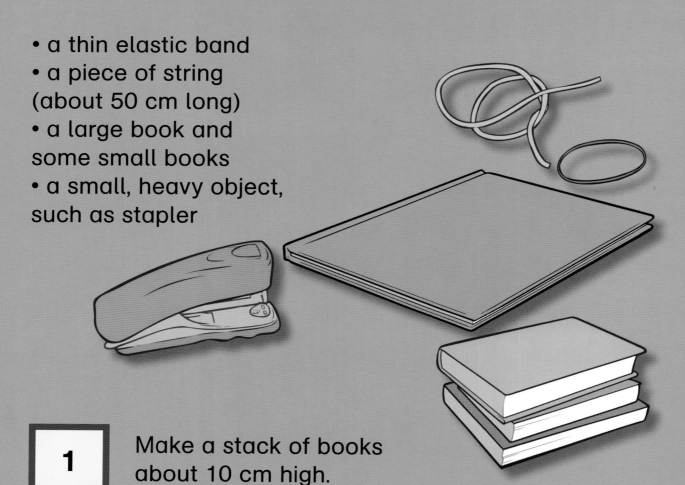

| 1 | Make a stack of books about 10 cm high. |

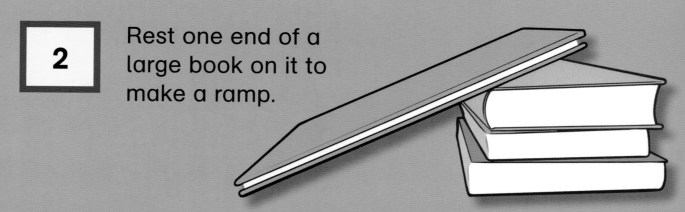

| 2 | Rest one end of a large book on it to make a ramp. |

3 Tie one end of the string to the object and the other end to the elastic band.

4 Lift the object by pulling on the end of the elastic band.

5 Now rest the object on the ramp and pull it up the ramp by pulling the elastic band.

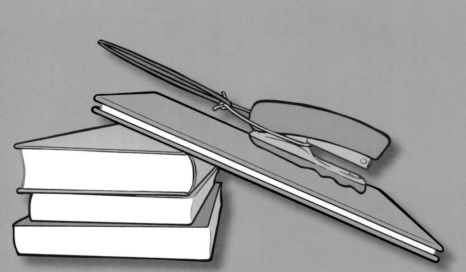

The elastic band stretches most when you lift the object vertically. The ramp lets you use a smaller pull to lift the object.

Spot the wedges and ramps

Can you spot the wedges and ramps on these pages? Try to work out what each one does.

Find the wedge. What does it do?

You have wedges in your body! What are they called?

Part of this boat is pushing water aside. Where is it?

There are two ramps in a playground slide. Where are they?

Answers are on page 32.

Words to remember

axe
A simple tool with a metal, wedge-shaped head on a handle, used for chopping wood.

carpenter
Someone who makes things from wood.

chisel
A piece of metal with a sharp, wedge-shaped end, used for shaping a piece of wood.

conveyor
A machine that moves material, such as crushed rock, from place to place.

digger bucket
A tool that a digging machine uses to slice through the ground.

dovetail joint
A way of joining two pieces of wood together. Dovetail joints are often used in wooden boxes and furniture.

forces
Pushes or pulls.

hammer
A simple tool used for banging in nails and
also for pulling them out of wood.

plough
A wedge-shaped tool for churning up the soil
in fields, ready for new crops to be planted.

pyramid
A building with a square base and a pointed top.

stonemason
Someone who cuts and builds things
from stone.

zigzag
A pattern that goes from side
to side in short lines.

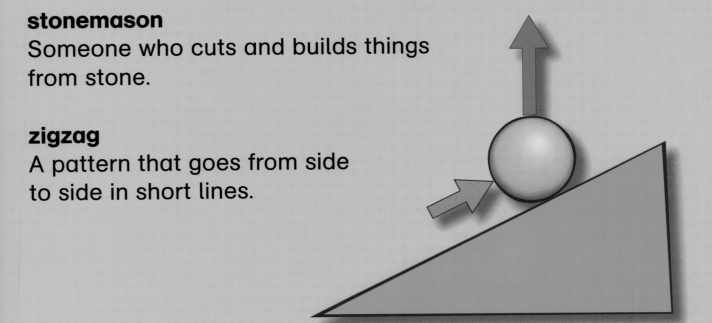

Index

Answers to pages 28 and 29

The wedge is under the tyre. It stops the aircraft rolling along.
Your teeth are wedges. They cut through food.
The front part of the boat is a wedge that pushes through the water.
The steps on a slide are a ramp. So is the slide.